Shifted Masterpiece

A Story of Love and Horror in Savannah, GA

VEE SPEAKLIFE

VEE SPEAKLIFE

All rights reserved. No part of this book may be reproduced, distributed, stored, or transmitted in any form or by any means, including photocopying, recording, or other electronic or mechanical methods, or otherwise, without the prior written permission of the publisher, except in the case of brief quotations embodied in critical reviews and certain other noncommercial uses permitted by copyright law. For permission requests, write to the author, addressed "Attention: Permissions," at the address below.

Unless otherwise noted, all Scripture quotations are from the King James Version and New Living Translation of the Holy Bible.

Vee Speaklife
5220 Jimmy Lee Smith Parkway
Suite 104-139
Hiram, GA 30141

Copyright © 2018 VEE SPEAKLIFE
All rights reserved.
ISBN-13: 978-1721731800
ISBN-10: 1721731806

SHIFTED MASTERPIECE

Nyota,

    Meeting you has been an absolutely amazing experience from beginning to end. Thank you so much for having such a sweet spirit and gentle nature. Every time I see you, you make me smile. On top of that you continue to support me in all that I do. Please continue to rock out this amazing journey of life and help me share with the amazing others you encounter what it means to be a "Shifted Masterpiece."

                      Peace & Blessings
                      Beautiful Queen,

"Speak Life, Not Strife"

VEE SPEAKLIFE

Dedication

This book is dedicated to my mother and any person that has ever experienced and lived through a storm.

VEE SPEAKLIFE

Table of Contents

1 The Beginning of the End.. 1

2 Nice To Meet You 7

3 Punch Anyone 15

4 Money Bags 25

5 Life Flashing...43

6 General Hospital..55

7 No Judgement Zone..69

8 Shrink Wrap...79

9 Puzzle Pieces..85

10 Shifted Masterpiece..91

VEE SPEAKLIFE

ACKNOWLEDGEMENTS

I would like to thank my number one fans: my son, my parents, and my siblings. I also want to thank a few people that have helped me along the way: Tameka Palmer, Sheva Quinn, DeAndrea Byrd, Keith L. Brown, Jessica Houston, Steven Hunt, Nadia Sanguinetti-Plunkett, Vele Keyta Redding, Veronica Ashley-Reid, Trudy Coarde, Jan Berry, Eloise Hudgins, and Clifford McGrady. To everyone that has supported me on this journey, named and unnamed, you know who you are; thank you.

VEE SPEAKLIFE

PROLOGUE

Some people are able to carry a secret to the grave. I kept a secret for a long time; I wouldn't tell anyone my secret. I have my reasons and my plan was to take my secret to my grave. Then death got in the way.

CHAPTER 1
The Beginning of the End

VEE SPEAKLIFE

I don't really know where to begin. It is a bit difficult because I don't really know how it all started in the first place. I only know that since I left, my life has not been the same from the first moment I locked myself and my son in the car, raised the garage door, started the car, put the car in reverse, and sped away. I was afraid for our lives and was completely uncertain of what would happen next.

I proceeded out of our development, a beautiful gated community located off the marshlands on the Southside of Savannah, GA. I had my son, his book bag, two of his school uniforms, my cell phone, my purse, and my work laptop. He was in his pajamas when I scooped him out of his bed and put him in the car. I was wearing a pair of jeans, a sweatshirt, and a pair of sneakers with no socks, no panties, and no bra. It was the quickest thing I could grab to clothe my body.

He said, in the sweetest and sleepiest voice you could imagine "Mommy. Where are we going?" Sadly, I had to pause and think because I really didn't know where we were going. It was around 11:30 at night. What could I possibly say to him that would make sense? I didn't have much cash and I didn't want to put any more debt on the credit card. The credit cards were already close to their limits. So I knew we weren't going to be able to stay in a hotel. I'm trying to think and not cry in front of my five year old son. At least with him in the backseat and with it being dark outside, he won't see these tears falling down my face. Think on your feet and respond to him. I heard the Holy Spirit say go to your mother's house. "Go back to sleep baby. We're going to your grandmother's house. Would you like to see her?" "Yes", he responded with excitement!

So, we made it to the other side of the gate and headed down the road to my mom's house. I called her as I didn't want her to be alarmed since it was close to midnight. "Mommy". "Hey there." "Can me and Elijah spend the night with you tonight" "Yes", she said in a way to reassure me that I never have to ask. "Of course you can!" "Thank you Mommy. We will be there in a few minutes." "Okay."

Thankfully, my mom only lived a few minutes away from us. I was scared to leave but I was also afraid to tell my mother what was going on and why we were coming to her house.

When we get to my mom's house, I pulled in the driveway. I park the car and I looked around because I'm afraid I was followed. Once I built up enough nerve to get out of the car, I scooped Elijah out of the back seat of the car as fast as I could. Grabbing my baby and everything I could think to get before leaving our house. I make it to the front door and I'm still looking around to make sure no one else is around. It seemed like an eternity before the door opened. I was so scared.

The door couldn't open soon enough. "Hey. Give me Elijah. What's wrong with him?" She was as frantic as I was. She proceeded to her room asking me what was going on with Elijah. Pulling back the covers, placing him in her bed, and trying not to wake him seemed difficult. She was concerned. Thinking something was wrong with him when all along, it was not him. I proceeded to her bathroom. It was still dark. But it's my mom's house and I know my way around pretty well in the dark. I can't talk. I don't know what to say. I'm almost frozen. She asked again, "What's going on with Elijah." I eventually just turn on the light. And that's when she discovers it all. It's not Elijah that needs her so much in this moment; it was me.

VEE SPEAKLIFE

CHAPTER 2
Nice To Meet You

"You should visit my church sometime. I have someone I want you to meet."

"Oh really! Who is it?"

"It's a guy I think you would really connect with."

"Is that right. Why do you think so?"

"Oh he is so nice! He has a really sweet spirit. The two of you would really connect."

"So, you want me to come to church to meet a guy," I laughed.

"Well you know that's not the only reason." We just looked at each other and laughed.

"Well what time does your service start," I asked.

"We start at 11:00."

"Okay." "We'll try to make it."

Who knew that going to this church on that Sunday would turn into my Series of Unfortunate Events? Certainly not me. I was extremely excited to meet someone new. I had just recently stopped seeing someone else that I thought would be a match for me, but it turned out he wasn't such a great match after all. So of course when someone told me they wanted to introduce me to a guy, hey now, I thought this was my chance to get my groove back. But no.

After the church service was over she didn't even introduce me to him. I kept looking around to see whether or not there was a potential suitor for me, but the couple of guys that were somewhat easy on the eyes, were not single men. Just as I went to thank her for inviting me to the service, she greets me with a hug and begins talking to me about the service and asks me if I enjoyed it and wanted to come back.

"Yes. It was a nice service."

"Oh wonderful! I'm so glad you came. Stand right here for a second," she says as she proceeds to walk away. I'm thinking she's going to get the guy. Chiiillldddd no… she came back with one of the pastors. Now don't get me wrong, I'm thankful for anyone that thinks that highly of me to introduce me to the church pastor. But really???!!! Where is this she got me to come here to see? Well, just when I realized it wasn't going to happen, I smiled and began to engage in a conversation with the pastor. After all, she did take the time to speak directly to me. And that's what I get for going to church to meet a man!

As we were talking, a man approached us practically knocking my friend and the pastor down to introduce himself to me. It was the most bizarre introduction. He proceeds to ask me if I could walk with him outside. So I'm a little nervous, a little scared, and a little interested. Surely he's not going to harm me in front of all of these people. So I take a chance and go outside with him. He proceeds to "interview" me. Just asking me the basic "I want to know more about you" questions. He was shorter than me; he was just okay looking and, don't trip,

I'm not shallow, but his grammar was horrible!! But just when I think I'm done entertaining the conversation, the sunlight hit his face highlighting his nice brown eyes, and I heard the angels sing. That's when he asked me if I would like to go to dinner with him. I paused and tried to think of every excuse for why I was unavailable, but I couldn't think of anything. "That would be nice," I responded. "But let me make sure I can get my mom to watch my son for me."

I couldn't believe it. I said yes and now I have to call my mom. I was hoping she would say no and that she had something to do. But when I called, I told her that a guy asked me out to dinner, and she was way too excited about it. I know it had been a while since I'd been on a date but...well anyway.

I met him at the Longhorn Steakhouse on Abercorn Extension, which I would later learn was his favorite restaurant. I arrived first and sat in the lobby. When he pulled up I was able to get a better look at him. He stepped out of a really nice car; he was dressed decently, and actually had a pretty nice physique. Needless to say, I got a little more interested. When he walked in he said,

"You're tall."

Of course this made me laugh and to my delight he continued to make me laugh for the next five hours.

It was a great first introduction to a man I would soon call my best friend. For our first date, he asked me several times where I wanted to go. I wasn't sure. So I asked around. My sister, of course, knows all of the nice restaurants and hangouts in town. She tells me about a Jazz'd Tapas downtown. Who can say no to live music, food, and dancing? I tell him about this restaurant, and he makes the arrangements for us. I wanted the perfect outfit and I finally find the perfect blouse. It was a perfect fit for my pants, and sandals. My hair was long and curly and my makeup was flawless. My jewelry added the last final touch to pull my first date outfit together.

When the time finally arrives, he is a few minutes late. "You're late," I tease him pretending to be upset but then I smile, laugh, and tell him I'm just kidding; I was really happy to see him. He then asks to use the restroom. He comes out and then I go in to find the fragrance oil from the room's air freshener from Bath and Body Works leaking. There's a small puddle of oil right at the sink. Shocked to see this, I try to clean it up and explain to him I would be out shortly. As soon as I was done cleaning it up, I tell him what happened, to learn later that he was the one to break it. I was determined not to let this ruin the day.

We ended up going bowling, playing in the arcade, and ending the evening at Jazz'd Tapas. I had so much fun. We smiled and laughed the entire time. He even serenaded me on the way home. He was the perfect gentleman; opening the doors for me throughout the evening and walking me to the door once we got home. We embraced, and he didn't even try to kiss me. I think I have a keeper in this guy.

He continued to ask me out. He wanted to see me every weekend. I wanted to see him too. It eventually progressed to seeing him a few times during the week to seeing each other every day. We were inseparable.

I was deeply in love with this man. He was charming and fun. He took care of me. He opened every door for me, he took me shopping, he never asked me to pay for any of our dates; he hugged me and never took advantage of me; he made me laugh and we finished each other's sentences.

We dated for exactly a year. I thought he was so amazingly cute, funny, and loving. He would always ask me "how long has it been?" Before I could respond, he would always tell me how many days and months had passed since we met. I thought it was the most romantic thing. This of course won him the biggest kiss every time and I was constantly singing the hook to Anthony Hamilton's "So in Love with You." It was an exciting, fun-filled, chivalrous, courtly, and romantic introduction to the man who swept me off my feet and called me his queen.

CHAPTER 3
Punch Anyone

One day, he asked me and Elijah to come over. Of course he didn't have to ask me twice. We made it to his place and when it came to a decent time to leave, he did not want us to leave; nor did I want us to go. So we didn't. I felt so comfortable and safe. The next day, I took Elijah to school, and he surprised me and came in for lunch. I began to prepare something for him to eat. I went to grab food out of the refrigerator and turned around and almost tripped up over him. There he was on one knee holding a beautiful engagement ring. My heart dropped. He asked me to marry him, and I excitedly said,

"YESSSSS!"

Then he says, "Okay. Let's go."

"Go where," I asked.

He responds, "Let's go and get married."

I'm in complete disbelief. He is ready right now - today? Wow. I'm floating on air in amazement and joy. We left his apartment and went straight to the courthouse around 12:30 PM. We had a marriage license by 2:00 PM.

We then found a family friend to marry us. He called his mom and I called my mom and siblings. My siblings and mom couldn't believe it. Nor could I for that matter.

My mom met me at the Oglethorpe Mall and helped me find a white dress. Lucky for us, it was June. There would be plenty of white from which we could choose. We (she) finally found the perfect outfit in Macy's. I love shopping in there. You can always find something to wear in Macy's. No matter your budget, style, size, or gender, Macy's has something for you. My mom chose a simple casual summer two piece set that I could dress up or down. We then headed to my favorite jewelry store across the hall in the mall. Charming Charlie's was sure to have more than enough variety for me to make the perfect selection. Sure enough, I found it all right there. We leave there and go to the beauty supply store so I can make sure my hair is beyond perfect. My mom and sister helped me get dressed.

It was a Thursday night, it was fast, and I was oh so happy. Everyone was there to support our official ceremony THAT NIGHT, and it was amazingly beautiful. I met the minister in his office, and he talked to me briefly. He said to me, "I know this is fast but I love that you still want this to be as traditional as possible." I played the song he would play for me every day as he would tell me how much he loved me. He opened the door and entered the room where my love, his mother, my mother, my son, my sister, and my brother were all standing there smiling. The sound of Donnie McClurkin's "When You Love" filled the room. As CeCe Winans began to sing, I entered the room. I thought he was so handsome and I could feel God's presence in the room. We held hands and gazed at each other. I could not believe any of this. I was filled with joy. We exchanged traditional vows and the minister left us with one charge. He said he did not have any divorces on his record and told us to not be the first and my now husband assured him he would not have to worry about that.

We all embraced as they congratulated us. Now it was time for us to celebrate. Since we were in Historic Savannah, only moments away from River Street, we considered our options and finally decided to head over to Outback Steakhouse on Bay Street to celebrate. We were so thrilled to finally be together as an official couple. We even exchanged kisses and took a ton of pictures. For a fast engagement and shotgun styled wedding, it was the perfect fairytale story for me.

We left the next day for a quick honeymoon trip to Florida. We hung out on the beaches of Jacksonville but mostly stayed in the room. Imagine that! I really waited this time. The tensions between us escalated up to the day we got married. It was great because I was SO in love. Every night during the week and at least three times a day on the weekend. Our passion and energies matched!

After two months of an amazing honeymoon period, we were scheduled to leave one morning to close on the house I had on the market. He did not sleep at all the night before. I packed. He did not pack. He started getting dressed and was just acting weird the entire morning. Then he tells me he has to take care of something at the school for his daughter. I'm all for it but he had a horrible attitude about it. He just seemed angry and I didn't know why. I had never seen him like this before. I went to try and console him but he pushed me out of the way instead. This broke me. He left shortly after that around 8:00 AM.

10:00, 11:00, 12:00 arrives and now I'm getting antsy because we should have left for this trip already to avoid traffic. So I called and there was no answer. I called again. There is no answer. 1:00 and there is no answer and no returned phone call. 2:00, 3:00, nothing. I am worried and scared. 4:00 I hear the keys in the front door. The door opens. It's him. I looked at him. He looked at me. I run to give him a hug but he barely hugs me back. I ask if everything is okay. Everything was fine. I told him I was calling him. He didn't respond. After a few moments he asks if I'm ready to go. Well now I'm pissed and rightly so. By then I put a few things in his bag but, he still needed to finish his own packing.

For an eight hour road trip, we were leaving wayyyy too late to start. Because he didn't sleep the night before that means he also prevented me from sleeping. Both of us can't be sleepy for this trip. He was not going to let me drive, but he did not know where he was going. This means I'm going to have to stay awake the entire time. I'm hot! We don't leave to get on the road until ~5:30 and as soon as we hit the highway, we hit TRAFFIC. So I give him the silent treatment as we inch along heading North on I-95. He now wants to be all jolly. Now he wants to talk. I refuse to say anything to him. This goes on for two hours and we barely move 5 miles because we were in bumper to bumper traffic.

The traffic begins to pick up and now, he's excited and I'm still upset. Now he starts to just poke at me and make me even more irritable. So I blow up. "Don't talk to me. Because all you had to do was pick up the phone and respond to my phone calls. Text or something. Then you have the audacity to have an attitude with me when you leave the house and when you get back" and bleeeeeeeeeeeeep @$&% reader fills in the blanks here. I remember using quite a few expletives and pointing my finger on his temple. That's when he politely and calmly slows the car down. He drives over to the emergency lane and stops the car. He leans toward me, and I begin to think of the first time he kissed me.

We shared our first kiss after a few months of dating as he respected my wish to wait. I really wanted to wait because for every other relationship I'd been in, I didn't wait. I did everything the wrong way with everyone else. Now, I finally get a chance to show God that I can have self-control and that I love him more; so I waited. I thought my reward for obedience was going to be my happily ever after with my husband.

As he moved in closer toward me I relaxed a bit and forgot about everything that happened that day. He looks at me. I look at him. I smile at him. He moves even closer and is now right in my face. I close my eyes and prepare for his lips to touch and caress my lips. I can feel him breathing and I'm ready to stop being mad. And that's when I hear loud bang and could feel the result of him head butting me. I hear him yelling at me and saying not to ever put my hands to his head like that ever again. I'm shocked and still. My face hurts and I'm silent. I'm speechless. As soon as I get ready to ask him why, he head butts me again but this time I was able to block my face a little. I scream and ask why and he head butts me a third time and I block again. As I am screaming for him to stop, he moves back to his seat and I notice blood on my hands. My head really hurts and now I'm trying to figure out the source of all this blood. I looked over at him and I see it. It wasn't my blood. His face is streaming with a flood of blood dripping all over his face. He head butted me so hard that when I blocked, my wedding ring stabbed him in his forehead.

Now, I have traveled to nearly every state in this country. He had barely been away from Savannah and had only visited the three places I took him. Before this incident, I loved the thought of me being able to be the one to show him the world. I've had many layovers and delayed flights. I recall sitting on a tarmac for five hours once. Another time, I left the country and customs security gave me a really hard time getting back in the country. Airlines have lost my luggage leaving me with no clothes to wear for extended periods of time. I have traveled with several groups and remember someone else in the group getting mugged. This was absolutely, the longest and worst trip I ever experienced. What was supposed to be only an eight hour drive turned into over 18 hours. Him driving many miles North then South then North again on the interstate. One time he fell asleep at the wheel and we ended up in the median on I-95. Of course he was angry again and of course I was scared. I didn't know if he was about to kill me or push me out of the car and abandon me. I didn't know what to do except prepare myself to "tuck and roll".

Late the following day, we finally arrive in time for the appointment. He cleans himself up and he apologized for what he did. I also apologized for "pushing his buttons" and we made up. He was wearing the biggest scar and bruise on his forehead. The scar was in the shape of a cross. The person we were meeting looked at him and said, "You look like you got hit with a frying pan." This made me nervous about what would happen when we left but I did all I could to make sure I was not the trigger.

CHAPTER 4
Money Bags

The next day and the following weeks were surrealistic moments that drifted slowly. I blamed myself for that incident. I never saw this side of him before. He was irritable. He was frustrated. He was no longer my prince charming. He was Dr. Jekyll and Mr. Hyde. We spent so much time together before we were married. But something changed. He became an animal. My prince ended up being abusive toward me. Even the fairytale of the evil stepmother and stepsister turned around to the evil stepchild being hateful towards me and my child.

What started as something that could have been a beautiful thing, my fairytale ended in just two months of being married. The excitement and fun ended. He pretended to be a person he was not. His words of love turned to words of hate and criticism.

My father was very loving towards my mother and my brothers very loving towards their wives. Of course I've heard them all bicker before but I never heard them put each other down. Who does that? I watched my uncles treat their wives with the utmost respect. Even as a kid ear hustler, I never heard any negative talk. My family is extremely loving. My cousins have all had long and loving marriages.

He even asked one of my cousins at our family reunion how did they stay married so long just a few weeks prior to this incident. He really admired them as did I. They had just celebrated their 50th anniversary. She responded that there would be ups and downs in any marriage. He did some things, and I did some things. You just have to learn how to communicate. If you can do that, you can do anything. Holding hands, we talked about this so much during our honeymoon phase.

Still thinking he was the best friend I ever had, that trip made me think of my other boyfriends. One of them tried choking me because I was getting in his nerves. I later learned it was not so much that I got on his nerves, but more that I just was not his type. Only one other did things that wasn't quite right. He was a former football player. He would tell me that I made him not feel smart. One day he got upset with me because he was having trouble getting our moving van out of some snow; this obviously was not in Savannah. He was getting frustrated so I asked if I could give it a shot. We both get out of the truck and exchange places in the truck so I can try getting us out of the snow. I cranked up the truck and we were on our way home. I beamed all the way there. He was not happy. Once we arrive, we start unloading the truck. He is still a little upset about what just happened. So he starts whining about it.

Surely he cannot be serious. What is the big deal? He wanted oh so badly to win so he starts making comments to me like,

"You have to decide if you want to be the man or the woman in this relationship."

Huh, what does that even mean? "You're mad because I got the truck out and you didn't. Now you want to say that? I can't believe you. That's stupid."

"Don't call me stupid."

"I didn't. I said that was stupid."

Charging towards me, he says "I told you I hate that word." He has now pushed me really hard against the inside of the truck. I push him back.

"Get your hands off of me. What the heck is wrong with you?" I storm into the house only for him to follow me. I was so mad I hit the wall.

"Don't punch my wall."

"Or what?" So I punch it again. He charged toward me and pushed me so we begin to wrestle. I got licks and he got licks.

One other time he got upset with me over me asking him about another woman he was flirting with. I didn't like it. This time, I pushed him. He pushed me back so hard that he threw me down the stairs and knocked me out. When I opened my eyes, he was standing there holding my head and my hands.

He later began treating me like I wasn't in the room. We broke up a few times after this. Reflecting on this relationship, I looked at my mistakes. First, always make a man feel like a man. Second, never make a man feel dumb and Third, never hit a man. I thought this would work for the things to come.

Once I realized my current situation, I began to develop coping mechanisms. One of which was to pick and choose my battles. I learned very well how to not be argumentative. I chose my words more wisely and only spoke when absolutely necessary. I just couldn't believe any of this was happening to me.

I ensured the house was spotless; dinner was cooked; clothes were ironed; kids were dropped off and picked up on time, and the mood was just the way he liked it when he came home from work every evening. Walking on pins and needles became the norm. Feeling like a child all over again, I had to gain permission before leaving the house and to make any purchases. This was a major change for me. My wardrobe also changed. I could no longer wear heels over two inches, and my attire was unfashionable and ordinary.

After the first incident, there was always something. Many and most times for no reason at all. After the head butting incident, I tried to change me to accommodate him. Over time, I stopped blaming myself and began to fight back. This initiated the countless arguments we would have.

One day I sat in our apartment living room. I noticed some items that didn't seem right. I pondered what he said to me the first time I went to his apartment. He kept it really nice and clean. It was very nicely decorated; embellished with just the right pieces of decor. I recalled him telling me that he decorated the apartment himself. After moving in with him, I was trying to find something to match some tall floor sized vases in the apartment. I asked him where he got them, and he couldn't tell me. At the time I didn't think anything of it. But then, a while later, I asked him about some other decor that was on the coffee table in the same room of the apartment. He couldn't tell me where he purchased this either. I look at the tall vases, the coffee table decor, and other items that, after observing him and his lack of the sense of fashion, I just knew that he didn't purchase it or anything else in the apartment. That's when I realized he was lying to me. He didn't decorate the apartment. His ex-girlfriend did. I then got angry and unleashed the old me.

I call him and confront him about it. He admits that he lied to me and confirms that it was his ex-girlfriend's style that was all over OUR apartment. So I shared a few choice words with him and ended with "and you best believe that you will not find any of this stuff in here when you get home." I hang up the phone, looked at the things, and proceed to put the vase and the decor in my car and I carry it all to the dumpster. My lips were poked out the entire time.

In hindsight, I know I should not have done this. Sometimes I wish I would have sold it instead. Other times I wish I would have kept it because it was really nice. I was being petty and jealous. To make matters worse, I initiated a stupid argument with Mr. Hyde of all people. This was a huge mistake. Although someone else was blessed with some fancy housewares, because I was getting feisty, I still had to deal with the consequences.

Not only did I have to deal with the physical abuse from Mr. Hyde, I also had to deal with the stress and residual effect of the many blows to my body. I was beginning to become mentally exhausted. I've suffered mouth ulcers covering my tongue and loss of hearing during this time period. Namely while we still lived in this apartment which, by the way, was located in a gated community. I tried to leave one night, not long after getting rid of the items and after another exercise of me getting slammed around the apartment. I packed my and my son's bags, put my son in the car and left. I left with a really bad attitude. I was having my Bernadine Harris moment from Waiting to Exhale. Deuces bitches!!!! I start the car, pull out of my parking spot, and proceed to leave. But dog on it!!!! There are technicians working on the gate. One of them walks up to me and tells me that the gate is not operating. So I ask when they will be done. He says he doesn't know. So he walks away and I start crying. I sit there for about thirty minutes in hopes they would repair the gate and I could leave. But no luck. I was going to go and check into a hotel. I realize after waiting that I can't sit there with my son in the car. So I take this as a sign that I'm not supposed to leave. So I go back. Park in my spot and I sit in the car for a few more minutes. I couldn't do it, I went back just one more time to see if the gate is fixed. No. It's still broken. I do not want to go back in that apartment. I get Elijah and carry him back inside, gasping as I turn the key. Because now, I have to apologize.

Not long after I tried to leave, Mr. Hyde came home one day after work and was so frustrated that he started crying. This is how I knew I still loved him. I consoled him. I didn't want him to feel bad. He learned that day that he was demoted on his job. I learned that I wanted to be there for my husband and proclaimed this was why I didn't leave. He needed his best friend more than ever now. And I was going to be there for him no matter what.

Time passes and we eventually move out of the apartment and into this beautiful house. He let me pick it out and I was excited. It was a beautiful open floor plan ranch style home. The kitchen was perfect for entertaining. The rooms were split with this enormous gap between the master bedroom and the rooms where the children would sleep. There was plenty of space in the backyard. It would have been perfect for a cookout. There was a covered patio with three separate entrances. One off the kitchen, one off the living room, and another off the master bedroom.

He had full custody of his daughter. So his daughter spent every weekend and summer with her mother. Most weekends, my son would spend time with my mother. When Elijah was with us, I loved spending time with him in the mornings. He was so sweet. We would build Lego sets together on these mornings. Not only was it an outlet for my son, it was also an outlet for me; the weekends were the worst. I thought that on these days, after I made his pancakes and served him in the room, it would make a difference. His behavior seemed worse and tension between us escalated every Saturday. Each week I knew that I could expect some form of physical harm. Thankfully, the living room, dining room, family room, and kitchen separated our room from the kids' rooms. There was enough distance between us to muffle the noise. The sound of my voice was covered.

I used to fight back. But there came a time when I stopped fighting because it seemed to make it even worse or I would get hurt more. I just let him push me around and I wouldn't say anything. He no longer had any compassion for me. When I cried, he didn't care. When I was physically hurt, he only cared if he left a mark that others would see. I always asked why and he would always apologize and tell me it would never happen again.

One night after dinner, I decided to ask him why he was always so angry. I told him he changed and was not who I dated at all. He responded that he was stressed about the bills and I didn't get it. Life should be great at this point. Why are his finances messed up? When I sold my house he demanded that I give him half of the money? No. I WILL NOT and did not. He helped me stage the house to sell it and he thought that earned him a big time payment of half. No! I helped him pay off a few bills though. It was ME that purchased a home and paid a mortgage. So I paid off MY bills. I can't say my thoughts would have been different even if he didn't head butt me the day before I closed on the house. Regardless, I earned it. Not him. I think I was beyond fair. After head butting me, he didn't deserve anything. Embarrassment kept me from sharing this with anyone. At this point, he made me feel as though he married me for my money. Which makes no sense because our take home pay was about the same. His work benefits though were much better than mine because he had free healthcare for the family. As much as healthcare costs now and then, it was a definite perk for me but not enough for what was getting ready to come next.

After I asked him what was wrong, and why he was so angry, this time he says it was about finances. He was frustrated with HIS finances. He said he was physically tired and stressed about his finances. So I decide that I can help. We are splitting all of the household bills in half. He would pay his personal bills prior to us getting married and I would pay mine. Anything we incurred together, we would split this as well. I thought this worked well until he said he was stressed. So here I come, not only trying to save the day but also trying to prevent some more physical harm to myself, "babe, would it be helpful if I paid the bills this month?" He agreed and we were supposed to be good. The following month he asked if we could do it again. I was hesitant but I agreed. During this time he made sure that I didn't have any extra money. Everything I made was exhausted by the bills. This lasted the next six months and the physical abuse did not stop.

Now Mr. Hyde is abusing me physically, mentally, financially, emotionally, and spiritually. Now I'm getting angry. During this time, he fractured my ankles, fractured my wrists, and attempted to push me out of a moving car. One time I planned weeks prior to meet some girlfriends for a girl's night. When the day finally arrived, he didn't want me to go even though I checked to see if he were okay with me going when the ladies planned the night. Just before I am to leave and head to the restaurant, I take Elijah to my mother's house. Mr. Hyde comes to my mother's house unexpectedly and tells me he doesn't want me to go. I begin to explain that I won't be out all night. He begins to get upset and tells me how I'm not trying to make things work for us and that he knew that I was going to meet someone else. He is getting louder and louder. All in my mom's driveway. My mom's neighbor is outside and I just know they can hear everything. I also know my mom must be able to hear him inside her house. I can't believe this. He tells me I can't go. I argue back and tell him that he can't control me and that he was being loud and rude. So I walk away. He pulls my arm and tries to prevent me from getting in the car. I got in and locked the doors. He jumps in his car, cranks it up and blocks the driveway to prevent me from pulling out of the driveway. But me being a "gangsta", I drive on my mom's grass and go around him. He proceeds to jump in his car, speed away from my mother's house, and chase after me. I get off my mom's street and decide to get on the nearest highway. He is on my car tail so I speed up. He then pulls around to the side of my car and attempts to swerve and hit my car. He has his window down and is yelling at me to stop the car and pull over. Dammit...where are the cops. This highway always has a cop waiting to give someone ticket. Not today... I roll my window down. I pulled out my phone and try to record him trying to kill me. He sees this and stops. He gets off at the next exit and I keep going. I go ahead to meet my girlfriends. I sit there at the Melting Pot with my friends and look over the menu. I end up ordering my Cajun cheese and dessert fondue as I sit, laugh, smile, and pretend this did not just happen. My husband did not just attempt to run me off the road with his car. I was obviously scared to go home on this night. Once again, he forced himself on me. Once again, I cry until I fall asleep.

My birthday comes a couple of weeks later. The day before, he and his daughter apologize to me for them both being rude to me. I was numb to them both treating me like garbage when, through it all, I treated them both really well. I got up on my birthday and Mr. Hyde was already grumpy. I say good morning and I got no response. I leave and head out for my morning "walk jog." A few moments later, he catches up to me and starts to follow me in his car. He yells for me to get in the car. I tell him no. He continues this for a few moments and then drives away and out of our development when he sees one of the neighbors. I jog the rest of the way home. Just as I get in, I hear the car pull up in the driveway. He comes in and attacked me.

It was a milestone birthday and I was pissed. No he didn't. I was already making accommodations for him. I already changed who I was for him. I was someone completely different. Aside from the way I dressed, my behavior was different. I was quiet and less vocal. But are you kidding me. I'm doing all of this; he wasn't doing anything for me; he wasn't giving me anything (not even an orgasm), and he wants to abuse me every chance he gets.

I'm done. I clocked out mentally. I begin making preparations to leave. If I weren't tied to the lease agreement for the house, I would have left that day. I had to wait five months. I figured I could stand a few more months.

The abuse escalated over time. It went from shoving and slamming me into walls to punching me in the face. He no longer treated me like his queen, but more like a random dude he was having an altercation with during a bar fight, and I was always accused of cheating on him.

Do you remember *The Burning Bed* starring Farrah Fawcett? What about Julia Roberts' portrayal of an abused woman in *Sleeping with the Enemy*. J-Lo followed suit, as she did most of Julia Roberts' films, with *Enough*. Then you have Whoopi Goldberg in "The Color Purple", and Angela Bassett's portrayal of Tina Turner in *What's Love Got to do With It*. All stories depicting the abused and battered wife. Many days I had thoughts of God wiping them all out. Mr. Hyde burning in his bed; scratching his car like Bernadine or even blowing it up with him in it. I had many thoughts of taking control and managing things that were uncontrollable. They were all negative and none of them were nice except those that would keep me and Elijah safe. I wanted to leave.

But I also knew that my negative actions and negative behaviors would lead me down a path of destruction. I knew then that I needed to change my thought process and try to not think so negatively all the time and do what I could to make the most of the situation; the situation I thought I created. Even though I made the vows and didn't want to be in them. I still did not think it was okay to divorce; I thought we just needed to separate. Perhaps we just needed some time apart but the longer I stayed, the more tragic events occurred. Things became worse. The more I tried to make accommodations to his negative behaviors. The worst things became for me. I wanted to do better. I wanted to make sure that my actions were not the cause of my demise; not only here on Earth but in heaven as well. I was not living as holy as I could because I was so angry. Then there are days that I recall when I wanted to try to live right and do better. I then remembered a scripture.

The Holy Bible says to "Love your enemies, bless them that curse you, do good to them that hate you, and pray for them which despitefully use you, and persecute you" Matthew 5:44 KJV

So, I stayed.

One day I went to the courthouse to initiate the divorce process. I sat at the associate's desk sitting across from her looking at me asking, "How may I help you?" Now, I couldn't do anything but cry. I immediately burst into tears and told her that I wanted to understand what I needed to do to get a divorce. It was at that point that I realized that I could not go through with it. I could not end the marriage. It didn't seem right. I was afraid of feeling alone. I was afraid of being called a failure. I was afraid of what everyone would have to say. Afraid of the fact that I was over 40 and I didn't get married until I turned 38. I was afraid of all the things that they would have to say about me not marrying my son's father, having a new husband, and now ending this marriage with a divorce. Never having a successful relationship or one that I could call a great success. So desperately, I wanted to say I was happy and found marital bliss. Now that it was over, I wasn't going to be able to say that I honored my wedding vows. I was so afraid of the consequences of getting a divorce and of leaving my husband as a battered woman. I was completely embarrassed. I was exhausted but more so exhausted of the consequences. I knew that I was not happy at my home. Not only did I want to prove something to everyone else, I wanted to prove something to myself. I thought this was the right approach. I thought staying was going to be my saving grace. I thought that by me not asking him for the divorce, I was doing the right thing. I thought I just needed to get my affairs in order and that I needed to stop returning the meanness that I was receiving. I thought that would be the better approach. I despise the thought of being called a failure and I despised the thought of people looking at me as a failure. I did not want to have an unsuccessful marriage.

CHAPTER 5
Life Flashing

His birthday came and I planned to be sure he had a great day even though things between us were getting worse. I decorated the house for him and got him a cake. He didn't get home until late and he barely said thank you.

Another month goes by and blows to my face were normal. Being slammed against walls and chased around the house was normal. Trying to leave and escape the house was normal. It wasn't normal for me to want to prepare a romantic evening for us because he was seemingly nice to me that day. He wasn't calling me to harass me about not answering the phone quickly enough. When he talked to me on this day he was actually kind. It inspired me to want to reward his so called "good behavior" that evening when he came home.

Dinner was already prepared. I made one of the few meals in which he would give me compliments. It was one of the simplest meals. I was thankful for it though because it was always eaten with no complaints. He would also take it for his lunch. By this time I knew exactly how he liked it. Sweet with 3 scoops of white sugar, lightly seasoned ground beef, spaghetti sauce with meat and noodles all mixed together, and topped off with two bags of mild cheddar cheese. Spaghetti days were the best.

My son was all ready for bed. He and his daughter would be in shortly. I had a few things to finish for work. I had a huge deadline the next day and I tried my best to wrap things up so I could cater to him when he came home. Once I got to a stopping point I made sure Elijah was tucked away in bed and I went to my room. I turned on the water in the shower, undressed and got in the shower. I washed my hair. Smiling and thinking about us before we got married as I so often did. It was my go to happy place. Cleansing my body from head to toe, I felt fresh, clean, and ready to engage in any activity my husband desired. I wasn't going to cry on this night. On this night, I wanted to treat him more than well just for being nice earlier that day.

He came in as I was getting out of the shower. "Hey babe," I smiled. I was actually excited to see him. I literally had done everything but lay out rose petals across the bed, in the whirlpool bath, and on the walkway. He looked at me. I didn't see my prince charming. It was Mr. Hyde. I grabbed my robe, put it on, and tried to tie it. "Aren't you going to give me a kiss," he asked? I knew then there would be trouble by his tone. He was angry and I didn't know what to expect next. I tried to open our bedroom door because I thought maybe this would eliminate any struggle that was about to occur. I didn't want to kiss him. He was being mean and it was a complete turn off to what I was planning. I don't like Mr. Hyde. If I could avoid Mr. Hyde I would.

He again yelled, "Aren't you going to give me a kiss?"

"No. I responded as I quickly slid passed him and out the bedroom door. I knew what was coming next, as it happened so many times before. So I went to check on Elijah to make sure his bedroom door was closed. It was still daylight which was a little different. Most incidents happened after the kids were asleep. He begins following me around the house and I try grabbing the house phone.

"Who are you calling? Can't a man come home and have his wife give him a kiss?" I begin to ignore him. Hoping my silence would keep him from wanting to argue. He begins to get louder and louder. Following me around the house. I make it back to our bedroom with him at my heels. "Stop being like that. It makes no sense for a husband to have to beg his wife for a kiss." I remain silent and as calm as possible. I sat still on the bed and that's when he stands in front of me. "You're going to kiss me," he yells. He then proceeds to grab the back of my head, forcing me to kiss him. He smelled horrible and looked greasy. It's going to happen again as it had so many times before. He's going to force me to have sex with him. The first time I fought back. He was so much stronger than me that it didn't matter. I tried to fight the next few times but it never worked. Many nights I would lay there and wait for it to be over as fighting always made it worse. I vowed to myself while he was kissing me that I didn't want to be there anymore. He hurt me so bad because this was the one day I was trying to be nice. I wanted to be the wife and I wanted desperately for Mr. Hyde to be my husband. Instead, I fought. I mustered enough strength to throw him off of me. I flipped him over the bed. "Oh. You think because you are walking and exercising that you are getting stronger.

"Please stop," I scream. "Not tonight!" "Please not tonight!"

He and I both jumped up after I flipped him over the bed and we found ourselves standing in front of the chest of drawers. I tried to pass him and he told me I wasn't going to leave. The same way he told me many times before.

"I'm never leaving you and you're never going to be able to leave me."

He said this to me on more than one occasion and I always took it as a threat; after all, it never sounded like a term of endearment. As we continue to face each other, I thought of the different ways I could get out and away from him. He just continued to push and shove me around with every attempt to pass him. Just when I thought I could escape from the door that leads to the patio I tussle with him to open the door. He slams it shut at each attempt. He began to get tired and sat down. So I tried to escape again. This time I make it out of the room and scream for help. No one heard me. No one came. I could see my friendly neighbor's house. She was an older woman living alone. I scream again as I run closer to the gate. It didn't work. He was still faster and stronger. I reach to open the latch. He beat my hands off the latch and began pulling me backwards. I scream her name. He then covers my mouth with his hand. This gives me a chance to try and wiggle away. He pulls me back in by pulling my robe. Between me trying to run away and him pulling me in the opposite direction my robe is ripped apart and pulled completely off of me. I make it to the gate again screaming for help, all just to be pulled back by him and dragged back into our bedroom. I sit there unclothed. I can only hear him breathing heavily in anger. I get up and I go to the dresser to open a drawer.

"What are you doing," he asked as he speeds toward me and kicks the drawer closed, barely missing my hand. I make two more attempts to grab clothes to put on my unclothed body. He kicks the drawers closed barely missing my hand. This time I was able to grab something. He tussles with me. He wins. This time by snatching and throwing the clothes across the room. I move away from the dresser to try going to the closet. He yells at me to get out of the closet. I reach for more clothes only for him to grab and shove me into the clothes hanging in the closet. He then forces me up and pushes me back into the bedroom. Literally growling and biting at me in my face like a dog. I can still hear the sound of his teeth coming together as his mouth would open and close: even the sound of the drawer being slammed close still resonates in my ears.

He pushes me on the bed. I get up. He pushes me again, "You're not leaving. Sit down." Mr. Hyde was here and I was beyond ready to leave. "You're not going anywhere," he exclaimed. I stop fighting and just sit still. I think maybe he will calm down. Perhaps there's a chance he will bring my husband back. The man I married suddenly tells me to get up as I sit on the bed curled up and rocking. I'm beyond afraid. I get up but not fast enough for him. He grabs my arms and begins to rush me across the room. Then comes the sound of my body going into the window. The window doesn't break. He punches me in the face. "You think you're strong," he says punching me again. He slams me into the French door which led to the patio. This time even harder. This glass does not break. Seemingly disappointed by this, he attempts to pick me up and slam me on the floor like a pro wrestler. He picks me back up and tosses me on the bed. This time I bump my head on the bedroom post, a nice and big piece of solid wood. And this is when it happens.

I blacked out. I don't know for how long. I only know that this is when I have multiple visions and see a series of events.

I see myself as a little girl on the merry-go-round in the backyard of our now torn down duplex apartment in Lamara Apartments. The wind blowing across my face as I smile, spin, and laugh. I saw my aunt working at her church, St. Mary's AME in East Savannah, and me falling asleep on the pew; I never stayed awake in church. I saw my father carrying me on his shoulders outside of Belk's as we, my mom and siblings, headed to Morrison's Cafeteria as we did every weekend. My dad putting me down and telling me I'm too heavy to carry. I saw my grandmother watching my brother and me playing with a little chick he brought home from school. We were laughing and throwing the poor bird in the air trying to get him to fly. I saw my grandmother's funeral and my brother and I pushing my grandfather in his wheelchair. We were all laughing. I saw myself graduate from high school and college and me at my first job. Then I saw my son as a baby and I woke up or came to after seeing my life flash before my eyes; I'm not sure if I was asleep or awake or how much time passed between me hitting my head and waking. It didn't matter because then I see Mr. Hyde standing over me and breathing heavily. I woke up to a nightmare.

As soon as he walks away, I get up and attempt to leave the room. Like a grizzly bear, he turns around, screams out, "Nooooo," as he raises his open hand hitting my face, and, with his nails he claws out the inside of my eye, and scratches my face. I cry out in a big and loud scream as I bend over to hold my face. In the midst of my tears, he picks me up just to slam me back down to the floor.

He continues to say, "You're not going anywhere."

"Just kill me," I whisper.

"That's what you want me to do. I shouldn't have to do this. All you had to do was kiss me when I came home." He punches me in the face and continues to exert his physical power over my unclothed body.

Then it stops. He gets off of me and walks toward our bathroom. I'm in pain. Although my body aches from head to toe, I do my best to get off the floor. I must get out. I finally stand up. It is then that I realize I cannot see anything with my left eye. I look around holding my face. I wanted to know where he was. He was far enough away for me to open the patio door again and get out. As soon as I reached for the door, I hear him charging towards me. I open the door as he's running like a football player about to tackle his opponent on the football field. I jumped out of the way and instead of hitting me, he hits the side panel of the patio door. He then slowed down as the bump on his head swelled. This swelling happened seemingly fast. He looked up at me as I stared in amazement.

I didn't feel sorry for him at all. I told him to get his shit and to get the fuck out of my house.

"Where are we supposed to go?"

"I don't give a fuck. Go back to wherever the hell you came from." I walk to the dresser and grabbed a sweatshirt and a pair of jeans. Without any panties and with no bra, I put this on and I head to Elijah's room. I grabbed his school book bag, one of his uniforms, underwear, and shoes. I scooped him up out of his bed and proceeded to take him to the car. Mr. Hyde is still in the room. He doesn't say anything and I keep moving. After securing Elijah, I go back in the room to get my computer and phone. Mr. Hyde still says nothing to me. I raise the garage door and get in the car. When I did this before, he was not too far from me. I guess the elephant man bump on his head got him. I'm am in the worst pain. By far, this is the worst attack in two years.

CHAPTER 6
General Hospital

Once my mom saw my face, she couldn't believe her eyes. In shock she says "What happened to your face? Who did this to you? Did Mr. Hyde do this to you?"

"Yes ma'am."

"Why. Why would he do this?"

"Mommy I never know."

"What do you mean you never know? How long has this been going on?"

"Mommy I just need some ice." She leaves to get me a bag of ice and helps me clean my face.

I look at myself in the mirror and I don't recognize myself. I'm shocked at my reflection. Who is this? Now I understand the excitement in my mom's voice. Her reaction was indeed correct. I know now why she was fighting tears and was voicing the extra concern. My face is scratched up with my inner flesh exposed. My eye, at this point is completely swollen and I can't see. I can't open my eye and the pain is completely unbearable. My face resembled Tina Turner's face after Ike punched and beat her in the movie; like Sophia after being purposely hit in the eye with the end of the gun handle in The Color Purple. Who is this woman standing in the mirror? What did you do to me? Where is the real me?

"You need to go to the hospital." Nooooo. I'm not going to the hospital. If I go to the hospital, everyone will know my business.

"I'll be okay," I assured my mother. "I just need a minute to pull myself together." Was I that immune to what happened to me today? Do I know what has happened to me over the two years? I don't think I understood the magnitude of what was going on in my home.

She sits with me for about an hour. In this time she's concerned and catering towards me. Of course she wants to learn why I've put up with this for so long. My mom begins telling me about my aunt and her much older sister. She proceeds to explain why I never met her. My aunt was murdered by her husband. I never knew this. I knew my mom had a much older sister whom I never had the pleasure of meeting because she was no longer living. I never knew anything about her being murdered.

My mother finally persuaded me to go to the hospital. "But what do I say when I get there," I asked.

"Just tell the truth," she exclaimed. "The truth shall set you free." The truth shall set you free. They say that a liar will steal and that a thief will kill. What lies was I told? Though, the lives of others did not matter. They didn't matter because I was living a lie. I was hiding my truth. I was hiding behind the clothes. I was hiding and covering bruises so much that I couldn't even share with my mother everything that happened to me that night.

Not only did I not tell the truth about that night, I didn't tell her anything. She and I, at one point, started walking around Lake Mayer a few times a week in the mornings after I got the kids off to school. One time around the lake is 1.5 miles. We worked up to going around the lake twice a day. One day I struggled to make it. Mr. Hyde purposely sprained both of my ankles the weekend before.

This sentiment alone, "the TRUTH shall set YOU FREE," resonated and made me feel free. I hid the bruises for such a long time. Truth. The truth? I have to be honest and tell someone besides my mom, my truth. If hearing this lifted a weight off of my shoulders, can I imagine myself actually speaking my truth? It was indeed a secret I kept to myself and only shared with the ministerial staff I trusted.

Ensuring she would get Elijah to school. I dreaded this but my body ached so bad, I couldn't see, I was scared, and I was embarrassed. Mommy do you have any sunglasses I can borrow. I drive myself so we don't have to disturb Elijah. The entire drive, I swear I'm going to run into someone I know. Sure enough, I get to Candler hospital and sitting right there is another mom from the school. I can't turn around and I try my best to not see anyone. My pride took over all of the pain. My swift walk was slow, but I refused to show anyone that I was hurt.

I checked in and sat in the waiting area, doing my best to get comfortable. It didn't work. Then they call my name. The other mother looks at me, I look at her, and I pretend I'm not me. In reality, I'm not there. In reality, I really believe I'm dead.

"Tell me what's wrong. Why are you here to see us?" I remove the glasses and show the triage nurse my face. "How did this happen?"

I pause and remembering my mother, I finally say it, "It was my husband."

"Was it an accident?"

"No."

She proceeds to explain that she has to call the police. Dang it man! I don't want to talk to the police. Don't they see me looking a hot mess? Don't they know that will make matters worse for me when I get home?

After taking my vitals, she places me in a waiting area. It's cold and I'm uncomfortable. A nurse practitioner finally comes and administers medicine in my eye. This offered some relief. "What happened to you dear?" Not her too. I have to tell you too? No thanks. "It's okay dear. You are safe here." Ha. I'm safe now because there are people around. I'm royalty when others are here. "Don't worry dear. These are normal questions after someone is physically assaulted." I thought the opposite. It was more normal to be assaulted than to be asked about it. So wait - I was assaulted? My husband assaulted me?

While at the hospital, I have a maxillofacial CAT scan performed, X-rays of my upper body, forearms, and my hands. I of course have to take a pregnancy test. Please don't let me be pregnant. I took that birth control pill every day at the same time. I even added a reminder in my phone so I would not forget.

I was so focused on the fact that I could not see that I didn't realize my head was throbbing. I suffered a minor head injury, contusions across my body including my arms, wrists, hands, and back. So I was swollen and bruised, but thankfully nothing was broken.

My eye injuries included corneal abrasion and subconjuctival hemorrhage. The white of my eye had a broken blood vessel. One would think the pain came from this because it looks frightening. Not so. The presence of this blood is not serious.

This blood will be recirculated back in the body. The pain came from my cornea. This is the clear part in the front of my eye. Mine was torn. This is what caused the extremity of me not being able to see. The medicine administered was used to numb my eye.

Before I leave the hospital, a police officer approached me. He wants me to tell him what happened. But I don't really want to say anything. He explains to me that he has to take a report but I don't have to press charges. That's relieving but I don't know what to do. I just don't want any trouble. I tell him what happened. I also took pictures of my face.

They gave me a lot of paperwork when I left the hospital. I didn't read it; I couldn't see. I went through the documents years later and realized that it was filled with support regarding domestic violence.

WORK

I had a project deadline that was due to the company's Vice President the night of the attack. Because I was busy getting slammed into the walls and busy in the hospital, I didn't meet the deadline. This sucked. Because now I have to tell my supervisor that I was in hospital. If I had met that deadline, you should know by now that I would not be saying anything to anyone else about what happened to me that night. I was going to have to have an emergency situation to tell my supervisor that she was going to have to let her supervisor know that her supervisor was not going to get what she asked me to do. I don't want to tell them anything but if I don't, my job will be on the line. I need that job. I sigh, take a deep breath and make the call. Over the speakerphone, they answered. "Will you please take me off the speakerphone?"

"Sure. Do you have the package?"

"No. I was calling to tell you I was in the hospital. Please don't share with anyone, but I had an accident last night."

"Oh my God! Are you okay?"

"No."

"What happened?"

"My husband," I paused. "My husband um, my husband attacked me."

I didn't get in trouble but this incident caused me to have to do more work because I missed the deadline, they added extra controls so it wouldn't happen again.

Two days later, I'm scheduled to see an ophthalmologist. "What happened to your eye?" You have got to be kidding me. I have to tell you too? I didn't like this. I don't want this. I don't want to talk about this. Is talking about this absolutely necessary? So I pretend to not hear him. That didn't work.

He asks me again, "What happened to your eye?"

It was one thing telling another woman. There was something relaxing, motherly, and soothing about it. This doctor did not make me feel good.

"Did you get in a fight," he asks.

"If that is what you want to call it," I respond.

He had a bad attitude and I didn't like. But I remember my parents teaching an Abraham Lincoln quote to me that sometimes it's "better to remain silent and be thought a fool, than to speak and remove all doubt." But I also, at the time, did not know what was worse, my husband causing the damage to my face or someone thinking that I got in a street fight. I didn't bother to say anything. I'm glad I didn't. The doctor gave me more medicine, instructions, and said "I never want to see you back in here again." The pressure from wanting to cry was painful. The tears burned like fire.

FAMILY

My mom's a ride or die!!!! Who knew? My mom told me everything I needed to do. One day she came in for lunch and said, "Let's go and get your things." She drove me to the house and went in the house and helped me collect some of my belongings.

SHIFTED MASTERPIECE

Boys to Men and Kenneth Edmonds sang and wrote it best:

"You taught me everything
Everything you've given me
I'll always keep it inside
You're the driving force in my life, yeah
There isn't anything
Or anyone that I could be
And it just wouldn't feel right
If I didn't have you by my side
You were there for me to love and care for me
When skies were gray
Whenever I was down
You were always there to comfort me
And no one else can be
What you have been to me you will always be
You will always be the girl
In my life for all times
Mama, Mama you know I love you
(You know I love you)
Mama, Mama you're the queen of my heart
Your love is like tears from the stars, yes it is
Mama I just want you to know lovin' you is like food to my soul

You're always there for me
Have always been around for me even when I was bad
You showed me right from my wrong
Yes you did
And you took up for me
When everyone was downin' me
You always did understand
You gave me strength to go on
There were so many times
Looking back when I was so afraid
And then you'd come to me and say to me
I can face anything
And no one else can do
What you have done for me
You'll always be, you will always be
The girl in my life, ooh oh

Mama, Mama you know I love you
(You know I love you, you know I love you)
Mama, Mama you're the queen of my heart, (You are)
Your love is like tears from the stars
(Your love is like tears from the stars)
Mama I just want you to know (Mama I just want you to know)
Lovin' you is like food to my soul
Never gonna go a day without you
Fills me up just thinkin' about you
I'll never go a day without my mama
Mama, Mama you know I love you
Mama, Mama you're the queen of my heart
Your love is like tears from the stars
(Your love is like tears from the stars)
Mama I just want you to know lovin' you is like food to my soul
Lovin' you is like food to my soul, oh yeah
You are the food to my soul, yes you are"

I'm healing. I'm home with my mom and I'm feeling okay. I couldn't see but most of the unbearable pain had subsided.

At the end of the first week and just as I was beginning to feel a little more confident about leaving the house, my sister stopped by to visit, "What the hell is wrong with your face." I'm speechless. I decide I will continue staying in the house.

Then my older brother and his family came to visit for the weekend. I was afraid to tell him and my other brother about any of this. I didn't want anyone to have to go to jail. We all sit in the living room and we hear the doorbell ring. It's Mr. Hyde. I scurried away to my room. Oh my God I think to myself. He had been calling me ever since the next day. I told him to leave me alone. I didn't want to talk to him. Just give me a minute to think. I couldn't think. He called me every five minutes begging me to come home. Text message after text message continued to come from him. I could not free my mind from everything that just happened. I peeped out of the window and there I see him moving things out of the car and give my brother something and he goes away. My brother came in and advised me to get a restraining order. I didn't listen.

Unbeknown to me, as I could not hear any of the conversation, my brother made him get all his things out of my car and place all my things back in my car. He gave my brother his keys to my car.

About two weeks later, my husband came to my mom's house. He knew her schedule and of course came there when she was not home. Again, begging me to come home. I wasn't ready to go back. He leaves and comes back on the following day. This time it's Mr. Hyde. He has that look on his face. I'm panicked because my son is there with me. I tell him to go to his room. I look around to try and get my phone. "Mr. Hyde, you need to leave. My mom will be here in a few minutes." "I want you back home with me. How are we supposed to work this out with you being here? You need to be home so we can work things out." I find my phone and once more I explain to him that my mom will be home in a few minutes and that he needs to leave. He listens. He goes away but I'm now scared even more.

SAFETY

The next day, I made arrangements to leave my mom's house. I left my mom's house to go to a shelter the next day. The devil is a liar. They had those little tiny roaches crawling everywhere. They finally put us in a room, and the mother next to us said, "Ma'am, you and your son don't belong here. He is too cute to be here."

I was a bit too Bougie or boughetto for this. But my husband kept coming to my mom's house. Where could I go? I left there and went to my sister's house.

.

CHAPTER 7
No Judgement Zone

I continued to work with the domestic violence advocates I encountered after learning of their availability. They helped me get the restraining order at no cost to me and led me to the attorney that would ultimately prepare the paperwork for my separation and divorce. The advocate even came to court to support me.

My family was also very supportive. They encouraged me every step of the way. My mother and brother even came to court with me. When I got on the stand, my mind went blank. I could not get the words out of my mouth. His mother and oldest daughter were sitting right behind him and his attorney. They all stared at me. Their eyes and faces were filled with anger and hate. I was so afraid. He looked like he wanted to jump across the table and over the stand to attack me. Although there was a bailiff, security, attorneys, a judge, people, all around me, I was still petrified. None of that mattered. That's how much power I allowed him to have over me.

"Why wouldn't you kiss him? Was it because he was dirty and just getting home from work."

"No." I couldn't say anything else.

My lawyer did his best to pull the words out of me and I just froze. At that moment, I had to recall everything that happened to me the night I wanted so badly to forget. I was numb. My attorney moved closer approaching the stand. In his hands were the pictures I took of my face the night of the final attack from my husband. He showed the pictures to me. Looking at my face sparked even more emotions. This time, it was more of disappointment and shame. My feelings were so hurt that my "husband" could, would, and did this to me.

I wanted to say I didn't kiss him because he was being mean to me. He came in the house yelling and screaming at me for no reason. He then continued to chase me around the house. I couldn't get any of these words out to answer the question. The only reason I would not kiss my husband that night is because he would not be kind. He came in the house and greeted me with an attitude and with so much bitterness I could sense another attack coming. It wasn't because he was dirty; I would have loved to kiss him and hug him and love on him that night and actually that's what I was in preparation of doing. After taking my shower I wanted to have a nice relaxing evening but there were things that I needed to put in order to make that happen. I was planning on having a nice peaceful and relaxing evening with my husband on that night. But I could not get any of these things out of my mouth to express. I could not share with my attorney as he asked me the question. I could not share an answer to the question because of all of the fear that was invoked. All of the staring at me. All of this was just too much it was too much to recall it was too much to think of and it was too much to ponder. I could not get the words out of my mouth. I just sat there in fear. I sat there with the anxiety continuing to build as each moment passed. Finally the judge spoke up and asked, "Is this you in these pictures?"

"Yes sir. It is me."

"Okay. I don't need to see anything else."

At that moment, I realized that the pictures I took of my face were not in vain. It wasn't because I took the pictures just to show off or to be in any type of way in my feelings. I heard God speaking and telling me to take a picture of my face as I was sitting there on the bed, waiting for some relief. I could feel all of the swelling coming up on my face I could feel every inch of my face getting more and more sore and to the point where is it was about to close shut. It was too much. All of this I had to recall and all of this I had to live over again in that courtroom sitting across from my husband and his so-called supporters. The same people that would come to me for assistance with things they needed. The same people financially or whatever that will come to me for anything they wanted me to do or to get him to do. It was killing me inside and I could not muster the strength to utter two simple words to explain why I would not give my husband a kiss on the night of this brutal attack.

As a cross reference to my attorney's questions, Mr. Hyde's attorney began to ask me questions. The one thing that stands out the most is his attorney saying that the reason for the attack was "because you were cheating on your husband."

SAY WHAT?! In shock and disbelief, that made me angry; that question made me even more upset. For him to have the audacity to tell his attorney that I was cheating on him!!! First of all, there was no reason for him to ever raise his hand to me EVER! AND now you want to sit in the courtroom and welcome this lie about why you hit me. When you knew all along that you had no reason. There was no reason for him to attack me on that night besides him just wanting to fight me. It was that he wanted to fight and I was done. I didn't want to fight him. I don't want to live like this. This is crazy!!! Who argues with someone every single day??? Who does that??!! So now you are going to sit there and tell your attorney that the reason you attacked me is because I was cheating on you?? That is really huge! That was the most demeaning thing that I ever heard! The fact that you had to come up with the biggest of the biggest lie and say that I cheated on you. Was that the best response you could imagine? You couldn't even come up with something realistic? Knowing good and well that I could not even look at another man without you making a big issue out of it. I had to hold my head down in most instances when I was with him. I could not even look at anyone because that would cause an argument. He had me so afraid to look anywhere or do anything outside of hold his hand and just stare at him all day. If I looked at the clock there was an issue. If I looked at someone's shoes that was going to be an issue. It was always something stupid. It was never anything that made any kind of sense to anyone. But because he could not think quickly enough, he actually sat there and incriminated himself. It wasn't that. HE could not, at that point, deny the fact that he caused all the damage on my face as he did. He was responsible for the image the judge saw in the picture. There WAS no reason for it. He wanted to make up a reason and say or have his attorney asked me "wasn't the reason he hit you is because you were cheating on him." I was not cheating on my husband and the craziest part of it all is that I really loved my husband and I was trying to do everything that I could to make amends to our relationship even though I still wanted to leave. I tried everything. I tried counseling with the pastor. I tried counseling with another Pastor. I tried counseling with an actual counselor neither one of us knew. None of these things worked because, at the end of the day, if someone wants to lie their way through life, you never get any truth and you never get the help you need. You can't get help if you are not honest. You have to be completely honest with yourself.

Even being honest with your loved ones would've helped; sadly this was not the case. He continued to lie all the way up to the time we got to the courtroom and he told his attorney that he hit me because I cheated on him; that absolutely did not happen. Mr. Hyde uttered this and I could not say anything. My mouth was open but no words passed my lips; not even, "no I did not cheat on him." He and I both knew there was never any time for me to cheat. There was never a time that he did not want me on the phone with him; all day, every day. I was in utter shock that he falsified an excuse for his deranged demeanor and behavior. Did Mr. Hyde lack self-confidence? Were his insecurities the prompt for him to blame me for everything that he did to me? None of this was cool.

I continue to sit still on the stand in disbelief, embarrassment, and anger. After seeing the damage to my face, the judge said that he didn't need to see or hear anything else. He arranged to have Mr. Hyde arrested and that was the end of that. I didn't know that would be one of the last times that I would see him. I only saw him once more at the next court hearing for his sentencing. It was the last time that I would have anything to do with him. He was now going to be placed into the system for criminal activity and domestic violence.

THE TREE

Now court was over and Christmas was quickly approaching, I was still hiding out at my sister's house, and she didn't have a Christmas tree. I was thinking that Elijah and I would have been putting our tree up with Mr. Hyde and his daughter if we were still at the house with them. Then I started thinking some more and started to get upset. I bought that tree and those decorations. Why are we then sitting here without a tree? I'm not buying another tree and I'll be damned if he takes my Christmas too! Let them get their own tree.

So, one night, my sister and I went to get the Christmas tree. It was a true Thelma and Louise drive by. Scared and crazy, we passed by the house to see if anyone was there. No one was home. So I opened the garage door. His car was not there. We were in the clear. I ran in, got the box and ran back to the car to put it in the trunk. Then ran back inside to get the decorations and ran back to get it all in the car. Closed the garage door and then jumped in the car and said LET'S GOOOOOO!

I don't know what either of us was thinking. Were we angry, selfish, silly, or rude? I do know that I was still hurting. They say that hurt people go on to hurt other people. Yes. I was still devastated. In fact, I couldn't believe that he would lie and tell the court that he hit me was because I cheated on him.

CHAPTER 8
Shrink Wrap

Making the decision to leave and not return took a lot out of me. I was seriously confused. If nothing else, we all had a great routine for our day to day living. Everything was calculated down to where we would be each hour of the day when we were together. So when Elijah and I left, I had to factor in all of these new changes.

We were living in someone else's space now. I can't say that I hated it because I didn't. I was extremely fragile and needed support. I was afraid of being alone but everything was still a daze. It was a surreal outer body experience and I needed to get back to me. Get active again.

I needed a desk to work, I wanted to avoid him and anyone associated with him at all costs. So one night I prayed and asked for help. I asked what could I do "in in the meantime". I woke up the next morning with a business idea on my heart. I started planning and mapping everything I needed. I couldn't believe that I started a business and was on my way. I started an in home wine tasting and online wine sales company. It was and still is so much fun.

But there came a point when staying busy was not working. Between my job, taking care of Elijah and, now this new business, my mind was preoccupied. I didn't have time to think about all of the bad and negative things that happened to me. It wasn't working because I was pissed off. There were no more tears. I couldn't even pretend to cry at this point. I was so ANGRY. The thought of him and everything he and his people did to me angered me. I was simply mad. So mad that one of my friends came over one day and said to me "girl your face looks BEAT." I started to respond "bitch, you can get the "F" out! I thought she was being sarcastic about my scar. Little did I know, she was talking about my makeup. I then remembered that I did go the extra mile in detail when I applied my makeup that day and "your face looks beat" at the time was the new hip term the kids used to say that your makeup looks amazing.

I was so mad and angry that my inner thoughts of my husband only wished bad things to happen to him. I wanted God to wipe them all out. Which is crazy because I was mad at him too. I didn't understand how God could make me go through this. I mean, in my eyes, I did everything right this time. Look, we waited to have sex before we got married. That was HUGE to me. Go figure, I thought sex was my biggest hang up keeping me out of heaven. So just when I finally think I'm doing everything right God throws this monkey wrench at my happily ever after. I thought I was closer to God; more than I had ever been before.

So you've got to be kidding me. I went through all of this?! All of it was done in vain? Someone please tell me the point of it all. When I couldn't answer this question, when I was feeling far removed from God, and when I felt that being busy was no longer making me happy, I knew I needed help. I was going to need to get help before I lashed out on someone or something.

I looked for someone to help me. I needed someone that didn't know me or him. A neutral party that had no knowledge of what happened. I wanted someone that would make me feel better but I needed someone to put me in my place too. So I did just that. This was a huge step for me.

One thing I learned after trying marriage counseling with him was that it is only going to work if and only if you are completely honest with yourself and with the counselor. It does no good to lie because the counselor cannot assist you if all of the help is based on false information.

I was not who I was before I got married. I didn't know who I was. Mentally exhausted, I was weak, hurting, and lonely. I even thought that having an escapade would help me feel better. But those moments don't and didn't last forever. Especially when their heart is also hurting. Two people just wanting to be held again. To feel secure and safe; to feel loved and wanted. It was a quick fix to an immediate need but this was definitely not a long term solution to being totally happy again. He had recently become a widow. We shared our stories. But the one comment he kept saying to me, "You can't compare your situation to mine." --- Please note that I never did. "You're divorcing. My wife is gone and will never come back. My entire house is disrupted." What he didn't understand is that no, my husband wasn't physically dead, and yes, I could go back. I didn't want to add to his pain. But are you kidding me? I wanted to tell him that at least he had sweet memories of his wife. I had nothing but a horror story. Although it's not a death, divorcing is very much like one.

Feeling inconsolable, I made an appointment with a counselor that allowed me to be myself. I was able to vent about all of the things that troubled me and the counselor was able to help me work through each of the issues in a reasonable manner. Sometimes I felt rather stupid for speaking about some of the foolishness I did but there were things I needed to get off of my chest. These were deep rooted issues that I needed to let go. Things I constantly blamed myself about on a regular basis. Things that I needed to manage like the nightmares of my husband and his family finding me and murdering me or my family. Counseling gave me what I needed to move on with my life.

CHAPTER 9
Puzzle Pieces

Love is blind and hindsight is 20/20. I was really in love with him. Even though he treated me horribly. I was in love with the man I met at church. The man that courted me, spoiled me, and treated me like royalty. Opening the doors for me and making it known that I was his woman to everyone we encountered. He was my best friend and was able to make me only see our world. I wanted to leave but I didn't. I wanted to divorce but I thought it would be a huge and unforgivable sin.

Divorcing was a really long process. It took three years from the time I left that night. Do you remember the minister that married us and also told us that he has married many couples; none of which were divorced? He charged us to not be the first couple married to divorce. Having this charge was another reason I stayed. I did, however, contact the minister to tell him everything that happened. He told me he would not want his own daughter to go back. He helped save my life.

After healing physically, I was able to focus solely on healing emotionally, mentally, financially, and spiritually. My sense of seeing was restored. After healing and after counseling I gained more vision. More insight on things I could have done differently and more actions were taken on my part to reach a place where I could forgive.

Because not only is walking away from the abuse, but divorcing, and picking up the broken pieces is also rather difficult; Forgiveness was probably the hardest thing I had to do. I did however get to a place of forgiveness and that is when I became completely free of the bondage and control my abuser had over and on me.

My fairytale did not go so smoothly. What started as a whirlwind romance and with him wining and dining me, him using every bit of his energy to make me feel loved, ended with internal and external scars. He lavished me with gifts. Giving me cards every month for our "monthiversary" and showing me and telling me how beautiful I was on the inside and outside.

I didn't stay because of sex because you can get that anywhere; sex is a phone call or text away. Sex with him though, was every night and had become a chore and no longer pleasurable.

It wasn't because I need to say that I'm married or to say my husband this and my husband that. It definitely wasn't for security. I went to bed crying most nights when we were together.

In reality, everyday wasn't a nightmare. Some days were actually good and reminiscent of when we dated. We even still went out on dates. I was definitely his queen on these nights and whenever we were in public together. I was always wearing the biggest smile. He treated me so well in front of others. Especially my family and our church members. But then it wouldn't take long for Mr. Hyde to show up when we got home. No one knew he was abusing me at home. No one knew that he disrespected me on multiple levels when no one was looking.

I wanted my best friend back. I was concerned about the flack I would get for not leaving sooner; for potentially putting my child in danger. People! No one understood that I made several attempts to leave. I was embarrassed. Ashamed of staying and ashamed of being one of the women you hear or see about with a man that beats her.

The last time he hit me and after two years of physical, mental, spiritual, financial, and verbal abuse and two years of me hiding scars and bruises all over my body, I left him with my face scarred, my eye swollen shut, and no ability to see. My vision was removed because he clawed and scratched the inside of my eye and I was left blinded for over two weeks.

Nothing in Hollywood, *The Burning Bed,* J-Lo in *Enough,* nor Tyler Perry's *Family Reunion* could help me understand the magnitude of a domestic violence situation. After this storm and experience, I get it.

Thinking of how I felt when my husband told me I couldn't do something. I would ask myself, why not? What changed from when we were dating and I got everything I asked to have. I could do anything I wanted and he happily supported me through it all. He spoiled me and made sure I knew I was his queen. Now after we married, I couldn't do anything without asking him if it is ok I could not go anywhere without asking him if it was okay to go. It was completely difficult to go from being an independent woman, to financially supporting your husband and still having to ask if you could do things that were not wrong. Things that were okay before you were married now not okay because you wear a wedding ring?

They say fake it 'til you make it. I was faking it all: smiles, laughs, happiness, and orgasms. But I learned that I was not alone. I learned that I am undoubtedly loyal. I learned that love does not hurt because God is love. It's not love that hurts, it's the obstacles you go through when you are in love that hurt. Through it all, I was patient, I was kind, I was hopeful, and I endured the storm.

CHAPTER 10
Shifted Masterpiece

I shared this story in hopes that it raises awareness to domestic violence and offers hope and empowerment for someone to move beyond the devastating stumbling blocks they faced when living in this environment. I Corinthians 13:13 says, *"So now faith, hope, and love abide, these three; but the greatest of these is love."* I still believe in love and I still have an insurmountable amount of love to give. Counseling helped me resolve my issues and helping others assisted me with getting over the hurt. Although I was angry with God, I know that my redeemer lives and now I understand and can relate to the story of so many others. I was able to move forward and live. I was bruised, not broken. I am healed. I am a Shifted Masterpiece.

Now that I'm done crying and God's wiped away my tears,
He tells me to stop and LOOK at what I have over there;
To see what he's done,
But to do it with no fear.

He says he knows the thoughts he thinks towards me
Thoughts of peace and not of evil
All to give me an expected end.
Looking up and not down
YES my child
You endured the storm and now it's time to finish this race
I needed to prepare you for more of my love and grace
He said all these blessings
Will come upon thee
And overtake thee
All because you listened to me.

Trust me my child
I'm about to take you somewhere
All because I'm getting ready to SHIFT the atmosphere.

Shifted because you changed
Created anew like the caterpillar that turns into a butterfly
Taking flight and completing all the things God has planned.
I am a MASTERPIECE
Putting all my cares in God's hands.

I'm now an advocate
Serving domestic violence survivors and
At-risk-youth in need.
Because God most certainly can
Turn things around!
I am no longer bound
But truly free indeed!

Although I was a little bruised,
I'm not broken
I'm spreading my wings and taking flight
Soaring through the wind like an eagle and
Gently landing like a precious butterfly

I AM
A SHIFTED MASTERPIECE!

SHIFTED MASTERPIECE

EPILOGUE

Now I know everyone has a story. The story you just read is mine; all of it. I know the symptoms are all the same. The circumstances are all the same. You may ask, "What makes your story so different?" Especially with the "me too" movement. My response is simple; it really isn't. It is however, raw and uncensored. It is a very detailed account of the horror and daily nightmare I experienced for two years and what I did to overcome the associated obstacles hindering me from living in peace.

When I came face to face with this storm, I did not know that I was not alone. According to the National Coalition Against Domestic Violence and the Center of Disease Control, "1 in 3 women and 1 in 4 men have been victims of (some form of) physical violence by an intimate partner within their lifetime. 1 in 4 women and 1 in 7 men have been victims of severe physical violence by an intimate partner in their lifetime. 1 in 7 women and 1 in 18 men have been stalked by an intimate partner during their lifetime to the point in which they felt very fearful or believed that they or someone close to them would be harmed or killed."

I shared this story in hopes that it raises awareness to domestic violence and offers hope and empowerment for someone to move beyond the devastating stumbling blocks they faced when living in this environment. Keeping secrets can be deadly and I hope the readers of this book can now make wiser choices on the secrets they keep. I am now doing extremely well. My son and I have moved on with our lives and we know for us, "the best is yet to come." – Vee Speaklife

RESOURCES & CREDITS

VEE SPEAKLIFE'S TOP TENS

10 SIGNS OF AN ABUSER

1. They don't like the way you dress
2. They want to control you and everything you do
3. They take control of your finances
4. They treat you like a child
5. They talk down to you
6. They blame you for everything
7. They hit you, apologize for hitting you, and tell you it will never happen again
8. If you believe in God, they tell you that you are not doing enough to be closer to God (you don't pray enough, you aren't nice enough, good enough, special enough, woman enough, etc.
9. If you don't believe in God, they tell you that you just aren't good enough.
10. They make you believe they are the only ones that love you. They make you become distant from your friends, family, and co-workers.

TEN SPEAK LIFE TIPS for DOMESTIC VIOLENCE SURVIVORS

1. Don't blame yourself. No one deserves to be misused and abused. So stay strong because you did nothing wrong.

2. Grieve the losses but don't stay there so long that you become depressed.

3. Remember to "Speak LIFE, not strife" over your situation as you do your best to maintain a safe, stable, and positive environment for you and your children.

4. Forgive yourself and your abuser. This may be difficult but the longer you hold on to your negative experiences, you will internalize them and become even more stressed. Free your mind and set yourself free from these constraints.

5. Seek professional help with a counselor.

6. Call a domestic violence advocate to help you with pressing charges and/or getting a restraining order.

7. For any and all demographics, YES, people YOU, RESOURCES are available for people just like you; USE THEM.

8. Think long and hard if you ever make it out and if you consider returning. Most people that go back to an abuser end up dead.

9. Keep yourself and your children active and involved in something you love, something to help someone else and something you need. Sometimes we have to remember to play outside in the rain.

10. Many people will have an opinion about your choices. Guess what? They are allowed to have an opinion. Guess what else? Your opinion of yourself matters the most. Keep your head up and your shoulders back. You have nothing to be ashamed of. Not even the scars. If you can make it to the other side of a living nightmare, you are a survivor.

You are royalty!
Now "rock on with your bad self"
SHIFT your crown and keep it
moving toward your destiny.

SAFETY TIPS

Call 911
Call the Domestic Violence hotline 1 (800) 799 - SAFE (7233)

If you are in immediate danger, please put this book down and call 911 for help. Always use a computer in a safe place and remember to clear your browser's history so no one knows which sites you visit. When you are researching an item, go to the library to and use their computer instead of your computer. My ex-husband stalked me with a GPS tracker. So use caution just in case your electronic devices are under surveillance.

More and more laws are being put into place to assist victims of abuse. Do not be afraid. They can help you. It is okay to get the law involved.

Stay physically fit and ready to defend yourself if needed.

Even though it made my husband more upset with me because I was losing weight and exercising more, being somewhat physically fit reduced some of the impact of the physical abuse. I was faster and quicker. I was actually trying to "get my sexy back" and do acrobatic moves in the bedroom hoping this would impress him. This made him angrier with me. He would talk down to me and say that I would never be the size I wanted. He liked me the way I was and that I was trying to get fine for someone else. If I could have attended a class, I would have. If you can, discreetly find a class being offered for free; kickboxing would be great. This may not only be helpful in building your strength, it may also be an outlet for you to have some fun.

Make an escape plan

1. Have a copy of all your important documents ready and stored in a safe place. (personal protective order, abuser's social security number, driver's license number, license plate, and your tax records, property titles and deeds, bank account information)
2. Do you know where you are going when you leave? (a shelter, relative's house, etc.) Wherever it is, make sure it's a safe place and a place where you can make a call for more help if and when needed.
3. Just like you give your kids a secret word just in case someone else has to pick them up from school, give one to a relative or friend to alert them to call the police for help.
4. You will need to have money or be able to borrow some. Do you know who you'll be able to ask if needed?
5. Just like you always have a bottle ready for the baby, always have a bag ready. I would have two bags. Hide

one bag in an easily accessible location and I would leave the other bag with someone you know and can really trust. You will want to put extra clothes, money, important document copies, and an extra set of keys in these bags.

6. You need a private or secret savings account in your name only.

RESOURCES & CREDITS

National Domestic Violence Hotline at 1-800-799-7233 (SAFE)
www.thehotline.org

Find local domestic violence programs here:
www.domesticshelters.org

National Dating Abuse Helpline
1-866-331-9474
www.loveisrespect.org

Americans Overseas Domestic Violence Crisis Center
International Toll-Free (24/7)
1-866-USWOMEN (879-6636)
www.866uswomen.org

National Child Abuse Hotline/Childhelp
1-800-4-A-CHILD (1-800-422-4453)
www.childhelp.org

National Sexual Assault Hotline
1-800-656-4673 (HOPE)
www.rainn.org

National Suicide Prevention Lifeline
1-800-273-8255 (TALK)
www.suicidepreventionlifeline.org

National Center for Victims of Crime
1-202-467-8700
www.victimsofcrime.org
National Human Trafficking Resource Center/Polaris Project
Call: 1-888-373-7888 | Text: HELP to BeFree (233733)
www.polarisproject.org

National Network for Immigrant and Refugee Rights
1-510-465-1984
www.nnirr.org

National Coalition for the Homeless
1-202-737-6444
www.nationalhomeless.org

Shifted Masterpiece Incorporated
www.shiftedmasterpiece.org

TEENS
Love is respect
Hotline: 1-866-331-9474
www.loveisrespect.org

Break the Cycle
202-824-0707
www.breakthecycle.org

CHILDREN

Childhelp USA/National Child Abuse Hotline
1-800-422-4453
www.childhelpusa.org

Children's Defense Fund
202-628-8787
www.childrensdefense.org
Child Welfare League of America
202-638-2952
www.cwla.org

National Council on Juvenile and Family Court Judges
Child Protection and Custody/Resource Center on Domestic Violence
1-800-527-3233
www.ncjfcj.org

Center for Judicial Excellence
info@centerforjudicialexcellence.org
www.centerforjudicialexcellence.org

National Coalition Against Domestic Violence
www.ncadv.org

Songwriter: Kenneth Edmonds
A Song for Mama lyrics © Sony/ATV Music Publishing LLC, Fox Music, Inc.

Book Cover: Vee Speaklife
Photographs: Courtney Bush Photos
Franklin Brown Small Business Connections

About The Author

With a global motto- "The more we speak life, the more we will see positive outcomes manifest" - Vibrant Vee Speaklife, is a sincere servant leader whose message is "Speak LIFE, not strife." The former Science and Math Educator is equipped with over two decades of combined professional experience working in corporate America and enhancing the lives of youth and families. She is now all about developing chemistry with the masses and showing domestic violence survivors how to thrive and gain positive self-awareness, worth, and empowerment. As the Founder and Executive Director of Shifted Masterpiece, Inc., a 501(c)3 non-profit organization that serves and supports domestic violence survivors, families, and at-risk youth, Vee Speaklife is a change agent who teaches Life Skills, Leadership, Anti-bullying Awareness and Legacy building.

Available for your event, Vec Speaklife's interactive workshops and keynote speaking topics include the following:

Domestic Violence
Conquering Fear
Unleashing the Hurt
Shifting the Atmosphere

Personal & Small Business Development
Canvas Unleashed (Starting Your Business)
Freedom Express (Goal Development & Planning)
Fundamentals of Brand Development

Single Parenting
Crushing the Lifestyle
Raising the Black Male Today

Youth and Young Adults
Haterade Nation (Anti-Bullying)
Hands Down (Dating Violence Awareness)
College and Career Readiness

For booking information:
www.bitly.com/vspeaklife
vspeakslife@gmail.com

For all queries about Shifted Masterpiece: A Story of Love and Horror, please contact:

bookshiftedmasterpiece@gmail.com
www.bitly.com/shiftedmasterpiece

5220 Jimmy Lee Smith Parkway
Suite 104-139
Hiram, GA 30141

Made in the USA
Columbia, SC
24 September 2018